Ballroom

Dance & Glamour

Bloomsbury Visual Arts
An imprint of Bloomsbury Publishing Plc

50 Bedford Square
London
WC1B 3DP
UK

1385 Broadway
New York
NY 10018
USA

www.bloomsbury.com

BLOOMSBURY and the Diana logo are trademarks of Bloomsbury Publishing Plc

British Library Cataloguing-in-Publication Data
A catalogue record for this book is available from the British Library.

ISBN: HB: 978-1-47258-073-3

Library of Congress Cataloging-in-Publication Data
Marion, Jonathan S., author
Ballroom Dance and Glamour / Jonathan S. Marion
p. cm
Includes bibliographic references.
ISBN 978-1-4725-8073-3 (hardback) -- ISBN 978-1-4725-8337-6 (epdf) -- ISBN 978-1-4725-8338-3 (epub)
1. Ballroom dancing. 2. Ballroom dancing--Pictorial works. I. Title.
GV1746.M29 2014
793.3'3--dc23   2014001428

Internal and cover design by Untitled
Project management by Precision Graphics
Printed and bound in China

Ballroom

Dance & Glamour

Jonathan S. Marion

BLOOMSBURY

LONDON · NEW DELHI · NEW YORK · SYDNEY

*For Lydia Ungaretti and
Greg DeWet – whose focus
was always the dancers.*

Acknowledgements

This book was only possible with the support, advice, guidance and contributions of many people. Direct financial support for completing this project came from the J. William Fulbright College of Arts and Sciences at the University of Arkansas in the forms of a 2013 Summer Research Stipend and a 2013 Connor Faculty Fellowship. Equally important has been the access provided to me by numerous competition organizers throughout my research,[1] especially Wayne Eng, Ann Harding, Judi Hatton, Tom Hicks, and Thomas Murdock for their interest, assistance, support, and facilitation at key points along the way. Thanks too, to Yolanda Vargas for facilitating many important connections. My understanding of ballroom – and the role of image in that world – is forever indebted to the online community at Dance-Forums.com; the dress designers for whom I have shot (including Doré Designs, Designs to Shine, and Randall Designs); friends and expert informants Dawn Smart, Larinda McRaven, and Iveta Lukosuite; and most especially to my friends and teachers Felipe and Carolina Telona, and Melissa Dexter.

Already familiar with my more text-based scholarship on dancesport, Bloomsbury editor Anna Wright first approached me about the possibility of an image-based ballroom book. I cannot thank her enough for conceptualizing a book of this format, or for her ongoing enthusiasm and support of this project. Likewise, my thanks to Julia Offen and David Marion for key feedback regarding the narrative structure of this book, to Eugene Katsevman for assistance identifying dancers in some of the images under consideration, and to Rachel Chase, KayLee Scott, and Alicia Troby – students in my Ballroom Culture and Performance honors seminar – for their assistance searching Getty Images. Finally, and most of all, I must thank the dancers who allowed me to photograph their lives on (and sometimes off) the floor, and to the various ballroom photographers with whom I have shared space along the floor's edge. As I was starting my ballroom photography Art Caruths, before his passing, provided advice and encouragement. Chris Hanson and Alliance allowed me access to their events, and Ron Self was of friendly assistance when I first attended Blackpool. Access, advice, and occasional freelancing opportunities have come from Steven Marino, Dore Photography, DecaDance Photography, and Park West Photography. To all of them – and to all the dancers – I say 'thank you'.

Contents

Photographing Ballroom

The book you are holding provides a glimpse into the artistry and glamour of competitive ballroom dance. It is a sample of the dancing I have been privileged to watch and photograph for more than a decade. Certainly immense effort, frustration, struggle, and hardship often lie behind the dancing and performance. Similarly, as a competitive endeavour, dancesport (the term coined to differentiate competitive ballroom from its social counterpart) is not immune to structural biases and political agendas. I do not mean to suggest that these dynamics are not real or significant, and indeed I have written about them elsewhere.[1] Rather, this book focuses on the outcome: the glamorous performances that are the goal of all the effort.

How the Book Came About

Although this was not my originally intended direction of study, my personal life led me into a ballroom studio,[2] and I quickly realized how rich an arena of social and cultural dynamics were represented – including issues of art, spectacle, sport, ritual, competition, costuming, gender, and performance. First taking group and private lessons, I later joined my university's ballroom team, and eventually competed in an amateur partnership.[3] As my research took me from local to regional to national to international competitions, two things became clear: 1) the importance of performance to ballroom culture; and 2) the value of photographs for documenting, understanding, and presenting these performances. So my cameras got unpacked from storage and I started introducing myself to the official event photographers – explaining my research and clarifying that I was not a commercial competitor.

Photography quickly became an integral facet of my ethnographic fieldwork. Few dancers had a concept of 'ballroom anthropologist', whereas 'ballroom photographer' provided a well-recognized and appreciated role in the image conscious world of dancesport – and having an accepted role facilitated access.[4] With photographs, I had something of value to give back to dancers at competitions across the USA, as well as in Canada, Germany, England, and Italy. Soon my images began to appear in ballroom newsletters (*Dance Notes*, USA) and newspapers (*Dance Beat*, USA and *Dance News*, UK), various online albums, and in adverting for ballroom dress vendors Designs to Shine, Doré Designs, and Leniqué. Occasionally working freelance for dedicated ballroom photography companies including Park West Photography, DecaDance Photography, and Dore Photography, my images were also used to illustrate several academic books.[5] In each of these cases, however, the images were there to complement the text. This book is different. Here, the images have priority and the text is the complement. The initial sections of this book thus provide background on the photography and activity of ballroom dance. The remainder of the book showcases the magic in motion of competitive ballroom dance.

The Ethics

Serious ethical considerations[6] went into the images in this book. Every image was taken at an event where public photography was allowed (such as at the Blackpool Dance Festival), or – and most often – where I had explicit permission from event organizers. Similarly, when finalizing the image selections for this book, I went back to confirm with organizers and dancers that I had their permission to use images I had taken related to my ballroom research. Since image matters so much in a performance-based activity like dancesport, editing decisions were not taken lightly. While it was important to accurately show the dancing as I witnessed it, even aesthetically strong images were discarded if dancers body positions or facial expressions were especially awkward. This decision was not meant to 'fake' better dancing, but rather to recognize that such instants were often fleeting in real life, and that to permanently cement them in print would be far more misleading. A related problem, however, concerned using images from earlier in dancers' careers: these images too would 'freeze' levels of skill (and even partnerships) that dancers may have subsequently left behind. Recognizing

that dancers constantly strive to improve, historical images depict previous versions of competitors' dancing.

The Photography

Visual anthropology and sociology have rich (if limited) traditions of photo-essays – wherein images are considered central and not simply supplementary – but typically as articles and not manuscript-length texts.[7] Here, however, you hold a full-length visual foray into the performance of ballroom dance. While film, television, and video may best exhibit many aspects of dancesport's movement to music[8] – including timing, musicality, speed, and dynamic shifts between stillness and action – for all but the most accomplished judges, who see all of these things in an instant, other attributes are more easily seen in a still image. Indeed, still images display attributes such as dancers' postures and lines. Similarly, photographs facilitate sustained examination, better revealing elements such as body positions and tone, and the details of competitors' costumes (see, for example, Figure 4).

As noted elsewhere,[9] my aim as an ethnographic photographer is to create images that are more than simply 'good pictures', but that help tell a story. Thus, while I personally may appreciate creative framing and angles, as part of my research practice I have typically foregone more artistic interpretative images in favour of more documentary ones: prioritizing how the dancing would look to someone watching beside me. Likewise, in trying to 'show the story' I try to shoot in a way that uses some element of the surroundings – be it the lighting, floor, or audience – to help provide texture and context (see, for instance, Figures 6 and 7).[10] A related, and key, consideration is the emotional tone of competitors' performances. To maximize this element of the story revealed by my ballroom images, I wait for dancers' heads to be visible, eyes to be open, and expressions to be clear (versus in transition), deliberate, and matching the tone of the dance. And, since couples dance ballroom, I aim to take images where both partners' faces can be seen.

A final pattern that shows up in the images in each chapter is that while the overall quality of the shots increases over time – due to improving equipment, photography experience and skills, and dancesport familiarity and knowledge – the range of angles (such as shooting from lower down) decreases. I was in a serious car accident in late 2009 that left me with permanent tendon damage in my right shoulder. As a result, I had to switch to shooting almost exclusively from a monopod, greatly limiting my range of angles.

The Images

I started my dancesport research in 2000, and my dancesport photography in 2002. In the summer of 2013 I was finally able to digitize over 12,500 35mm colour negatives from the first few years of my ballroom photography. Added to my existing digital files, I had just over 100,000 images from which to select. With 250–1,000 images for each one printed in this book, selecting the final images for this book was a tremendous challenge. Instead of an image-based overview of the ballroom world,[11] then, this book represents a window into my participating observations within that lived world. It highlights dancers I interviewed, became friends with, found interesting to photograph, and were considered exemplars during the years of my research. Specific events that were regular stops of my ongoing research travels[12] and specific dancers thus show up repeatedly, as it was through specific interactions – whether with friends, key informants, or champions (or two or all three) – that my research unfolded. Rather than artificially trying to show greater range, though, I have tried to select images that best reflect the dancing I watched: images that showcase the art and athleticism of the dancers' performances and costumes.[13]

Finally, my postproduction – like my ethnographic photography – aims to show how the dancing actually appeared from my vantage point. Using this as a guiding principle, I have only straightened and adjusted the colour balance on many of these images, as these are both 'adjustments' the human brain would make while watching in real life. In other words, in aiming for minimal perceptual distortion, I have used technology to mimic the brain's capacity to 'see' straight even when one's head is tilted, and to adjust for light sources' different colour temperatures (e.g. sunlight, shade, tungsten, fluorescent, flash). Other stories would have emerged with different photography and editing choices and different image selections. Here, the selected images generally follow a chronological ark within each style, largely starting with the 'who's who' from when I began my research. That breadth soon gave way to depth, as certain couples and competitions became more central to my research. In order to highlight the dancing, however, I list the locations for each competition in the Appendix rather than in each caption. Likewise, all images are digital unless noted otherwise.

Photographing Ballroom

It remains to be seen how much longer I will be doing dancesport-related research or photography. The time and expense of equipment and travel add up quickly. Similarly, there seem to be ever-mounting challenges amidst the rapidly changing media-scape. Some dancers and organizers now regularly use images without crediting photographers – let alone compensating them appropriately. Likewise, where the cost of equipment keeps increasing, more and more dancers now want only low-resolution images for Facebook. Simultaneously, various organizers' and publishers' concerns about liability add layers of difficulty to using the exact same images dancers are so eager to see publicized. Still, what started with my dissertation research has become so much more.

At the outset, and as I first started to interview and understand the dancers, their results mattered to me – often deeply. Knowing how much work and effort the dancers had invested, I would find myself holding my breath, heart racing, as I waited to hear the outcomes of competitions that I knew mattered so much to those involved. With time, and as I learned and understood more about the dancing itself, the results mattered less. This is not to say competitive outcomes were not important. Rather, I came to

understand that the results were only one part of a much more complex arena of lived experiences.

Dancers train and compete for many different reasons. What counts as 'success' for one couple might not for another. Similarly, sometimes dancing well mattered more than placing well; other times the opposite. Indeed, the same dancer could be disappointed for having danced 'poorly' one day while receiving a good result, yet be thrilled with superior dancing – even to a lower placement – the next day. As significant as the placements was how competitors dealt with their results. Some were excited, some were resigned, some made excuses, some laid blame, some saw it as feedback or stepping-stones, and some as validation. Did specific coaches' or judges' matter more to a specific competitor? What about the audiences' reactions?

As unique individuals, each dancer brought a different balance of artistic, competitive, athletic, and performative interests and aptitudes to the floor, as well as different expectations, motivations, and experiences. Most impressive has been how some competitors dealt with adversity – that is, the types of people they revealed themselves to be when the results had not gone their way. More than just an insight into dancesport, then, the lessons I learned from observing, interviewing, befriending, and photographing ballroom competitors have broader implications. A culture in its own right, the world of dancesport is also a compelling microcosm of myriad personal, social, and cultural dynamics – from apprenticeship to appearance, from competition to cooperation, from pedagogy to performance, from spectacle to sport, and much, much more.

Paralleling modern dance pioneer Isadora Duncan's comment that, 'If I could tell you what it meant, there would be no point in dancing it',[14] much the same can be said of photography: If I could tell you, there would be no need to show it. As such, I hope the images in this book provided a taste of my experience of dancesport, including insights beyond what could be conveyed by words alone. When all is said and done, though, it is the dancing that matters. I have been privileged to watch elite artists and athletes from only feet away – and hope that this book conveys some of the energy, excitement, and glamour of competitive ballroom dance. Rather than trying to produce a book about visual ethnography, then, this book is meant to be a visual ethnography. It is with all of these considerations in mind that I present here, for the first time, a selection of my 100,000 ballroom images taken over more than a decade, from May 2002 to September 2013. Enjoy . . .

Ballroom Dancing

An Introduction

History and Culture

With roots in fifteenth-century Europe and the French royal court, ballroom dancing, and its associated costuming, has always been linked to social class and gender roles.[1] With France as the leading European power of the time, the formal balls and dancing of King Louis XIV's court in Versailles provided a model for Europe. The trends started at the time eventually evolved in two different ways: into the performance-directed genre of ballet and the socially based genre of ballroom. This association between dance and social etiquette[2] has endured as part of a well-rounded upbringing throughout Europe, with ballroom regularly offered in schools or as a 'cultured' elective alongside musical instruction, and as the foundation for cotillion programmes in the United States. Similarly, from the first unofficial world championship (in 1909) to the standardization and codification of acceptable steps (starting in 1920) a model was set for the 'proper' ballroom gentleman and lady, with competitive ballroom linking such models of social class and gender with competition, performance, and spectacle (as seen in Figure 1).

1. 1959 World Ballroom Championships.
Held on March 10, at the Lyceum Ballroom in London, with the Joe Loss Orchestra providing the music. Although the women's dress and hairstyles attest to the time period, the general structure of contemporary dancesport is already evident and in place: multiple couples competing simultaneously, audience members sitting right up to the edge of the floor, judges standing on the edges of the floor, and formal attire the norm for a world championship event. © 2012 Getty Images (Photo by Central Press/Hulton Archive/Getty Images, Editorial Image #153473431).

Contemporary dancesport – the term used to differentiate it from social ballroom – mostly takes place under the auspices of the World Dance Council (WDC), with membership from 63 countries, and the World DanceSport Federation (WDSF), with membership from 87 countries.[3] This book is primarily about the dancesport culture represented within these organizations. For most people today, however, familiarity with competitive ballroom comes from the popularity of recent television shows. Starting with the British television show *Strictly Come Dancing* in May 2004 – with popular celebrities partnering professional competitors – the same format was first adopted in Australia as *Dancing with the Stars*, and has since been franchised and aired in 44 territorial variations. The US version premiered in June 2005, followed in July by the first airing of *So You Think You Can Dance* – wherein dancers from different styles are partnered and need to learn routines in different styles each week – which has now been franchised and aired in at least 25 countries.

In many ways the versions of ballroom seen on television are not representative of true dancesport. Unlike the televised versions, couples compete simultaneously and do not know the specific music until it starts playing. Likewise, couples are ranked against each other, not given numerical scores. These differences not withstanding, the televised versions have broadly popularized the general style of dance, movement, and costuming. Whereas most people knew nothing about competitive ballroom when I started my research (the first season of *Dancing with the Stars* aired in the US just before I finished my PhD), now people know many of the dances and dancers by name – such as Julianne Hough, Anna Trebunskaya, and Kym Johnson (see Figure 2) – and understand that being a ballroom professional can be a career and not merely a pastime. Similarly, bringing the appeal of popular ballroom-related TV off the screen, various versions of *Dancing with the Stars*, *So You Think You Can Dance*, and *Strictly Come Dancing* all now offer a regular schedule of live shows and cruise performances (see, for example, Figure 3).

2. Mainstream Popularity via TV.
(This page) From left to right, Julianne Hough, Anna Trebunskaya, Samantha Harris (US *Dancing with the Stars* host from 2006–2010), and Kym Johnson attend the launch of DL1961 and the 'Samantha' jean at Chateau Marmont on October 4, 2011 in Los Angeles, California. A former elite youth dancesport competitor, Julianne won Season 4 (with Apolo Anton Ohno) and Season 5 (with Hélio Castroneves) of the United States' *Dancing with the Stars* before moving on to music and acting projects (including releasing a country and western album and leading film roles in several Hollywood movies). A successful professional Latin competitor (see Figures 52, 53, 67, and 69), Anna has appeared on 10 seasons of *Dancing with the Stars* in the US, including as runner-up in Season 2 (with Jerry Rice) and Season 10 (with Evan Lysacek). The only professional dancer to win two different versions of *Dancing with the Stars*, Kym appeared on the first three seasons of the Australian version, winning Season 2 (with Tom Williams), before participating in Seasons 3–9 and 11–16 of the US version, including winning Season 9 (with Donny Osmond) and Season 12 (with Hines Ward). © 2011 Chris Weeks (WireImage, Getty Editorial Image #128011827).

3. Dancing with the Stars 'Live'.
(Facing page) A top-20 finalist on Season 8 of *So You Think You Can Dance* in the USA and now appearing on *Strictly Come Dancing* in the UK, former World Professional 10-Dance Champion Iveta Lukosiute is seen here dancing Standard with Sasha Andreev (top left), dancing Latin with Season 6 *So You Think You Can Dance* contestant Ryan Di Lello (top right), and in a women's group number with fellow professional dancers (bottom) left to right: Iveta Lukosiute, Irina Bubnovskaya, Lacey Schwimmer, Anya Fuchs, and Emma Slater), all seen here via the 2012 *Dancing with the Stars* show at the Tropicana Hotel in Las Vegas. © 2012 Jonathan S. Marion.

Genres

While many categories get contested under the umbrella of 'Ballroom',[4] the major categories at the heart of my research – and hence my photography and this book – are American-style Rhythm and Smooth, and their international-style counterparts, Latin[5] and Standard (see Figure 4).[6] The dances in each style, and the order in which they are contested, are presented in Table 1.

Where dances overlap between Rhythm[8] and Latin, they have traditionally varied in technique and tempi (as well as very different basic step pattern and timing in Rumba). And, while the Smooth and Standard dances allow slightly different tempi, the major difference is that Smooth allows partners to separate from one another while dancing, whereas Standard is the only style where a couple is required to remain in frame throughout (see Figure 4, bottom right). Indeed, the name 'Smooth' is meant to signal the premium this style places on seamlessly transitioning in and out of Standard's always-closed-frame.[9] Rather than try and fully explain these different styles in words, this book illustrates the differences in grooming, costuming, postures, and performance. Just to provide context, however, a few more comments regarding ballroom dancers, costuming, and competitions are in order.

Table 1: Dances by Style[7]

Rhythm (American)	Latin (International)
Cha Cha	Cha Cha
Rumba	Samba
East Coast Swing	Rumba
Bolero	Paso Doble
Mambo	Jive

Smooth (American)	Standard (International)
Waltz	Waltz
Tango	Tango
Foxtrot	Viennese Waltz
Viennese Waltz	Foxtrot
	Quick step

Dancers

Ballroom dancers are both artists and athletes – simultaneously expressive and aesthetic performers, and highly conditioned and skilled competitors. Typically passionate both on and off the floor, they invest (both physically and financially) in ongoing travel and training. It is not by accident that the most successful competitors least exhibit their tremendous physical and emotional exertions. Serious competitors typically practise anywhere from two to five hours a day, separate from additional physical training and careful attention to diet. The most successful competitors train as athletes and performers, and have typically started training as youth. Indeed, some of the competitors I interviewed were in movement classes as young as age three, and had started ballroom as early as six or seven. While these were extreme cases, most world-finalist calibre competitors had begun their competitive ballroom careers by their early teen years. Many of these dancers cross-train in other dance forms – from ballet to jazz to modern – and stretching and movement forms – from yoga to pilates to gyrotronics – as well as having ongoing aerobic, stretching, and strengthening regimens, and specific ideas about what diet works best for them, both as general practice and when competing. The physiques seen in these photographs, and the movements achieved, attest to the hard won physical prowess of dancesport athletes.

4. Major Dancesport Styles.
(Facing page) American Rhythm, American Smooth, International Latin, and International Standard – as danced at the 2013 United States Dancesport Championships by: (clockwise from left) US Professional Rising Star Rhythm Champions Nazar Norov and Irina Kudryashova; US and World Professional Latin Champions Ricardo Cocchi and Yulia Zagoruychenko; US and World Professional Standard Champions Arunas Bizokas and Katusha Demidova; and US Professional Smooth Champions Slawek Sochacki and Marzena Stachura. © 2013 Jonathan S. Marion.

Costuming

Linked to the dancing are the costumes, which – from their historical roots to contemporary television, video, and competition – are always meant to impress. Spectacular by design, ballroom dress serves two intersecting goals, balancing:

- *Aesthetic impression and athletic performance.*
  Designed and constructed to enhance movements and body actions of each dance style, costumes must simultaneously withstand extremes of twisting, reaching, and stretching.

- *Individual presentation and stylistic norms.*
  While other dance genres often involve dancing a specific part or role, ballroom dancers compete as themselves. Costumes must therefore fit stylistic conventions, but also enhance a particular couple's individual look. One must 'fit in' (i.e. not seem out of place) but also 'stand out' (i.e. draw attention). This is primarily accomplished through the dancing, but always enhanced and amplified by the costuming.

Material choices and construction should allow movement without bunching, and provide structure and support where needed. Finishing touches – from eye-catching and movement-enhancing embellishments to the expected shoes, hairstyles, and make-up for each style – should enhance and accentuate physical and artistic strengths (while hiding corresponding weaknesses). Reflecting ballroom's upper-class roots, the man's tailsuit and the woman's full-length gown of contemporary Standard costuming – the most formal and 'covered' costuming of the major styles – presents a model of dancers as a proper gentleman and lady (Figure 4, bottom right). On the other end of the contemporary dancesport continuum is the often deliberately sexy stylization of Latin costumes – from men's form-fitting trousers to women's skimpy skirts and plunging necklines (Figure 4, top right). Some have criticized the deep tans and more overt sexuality of Latin dancing and costuming as inappropriate/inauthentic ethnic caricaturization.[10] Certainly there is a degree of cultural appropriation involved – ballroom samba is *not*, for instance, 'the dance from Brazil' – but artificial tanning should also be seen as a form of stage make-up, meant to help accentuate muscle tone and help dancers not appear washed out under competition lighting.[11] As Latin costumes offer less coverage, it also makes sense that more tanning would be involved.

Finally, Rhythm and Smooth costuming fall within this continuum (see Table 2). Rhythm dresses generally resemble their Latin counterparts, but linked to the style's more social roots, women's skirts typically bear somewhat more connection to everyday (i.e. non-dancesport) dress shapes and designs (Figure 4, top left). Similarly, Smooth dresses most closely resemble Standard dresses, but without the floats that could be snagged as dancers move in and out of frame (Figure 4, bottom left). For men, formal tailsuits in Standard give way to dinner jackets in Smooth, and more form-fitting trousers and shirts in Rhythm and Latin.

The end result of this costuming is that while dancesport generally reproduces the traditional view of the man as the frame and the woman as the art – i.e. the woman's brightly coloured ensemble in contrast to the man's black costume – the specific versions of male and female being (re)produced differ across the styles.

Table 2: Costume Body Coverage

Most covered
Standard (International)
Smooth (American)
Rhythm (American)
Latin (International)
Least covered

5. Front stage – Backstage.
(Facing page) Taken at the 2010 United States Dancesport Championships, for me this shot epitomizes the connection between the 'Front stage' and 'Backstage' elements of dancesport – the inescapable link yet vast difference between what happens on and off the ballroom floor. © 2010 Jonathan S. Marion

Competitions

Competitive ballroom dancing is about ballroom competitions. As obvious as this may seem, it is important to recognize that the thousands of dollars and hours spent on costuming, lessons, practice, and travel are all ultimately about what happens at these specific events. Or, as I have noted elsewhere,[12] dancesport is best understood as a metagenre[13] of spectacle, art, and sport. Competitive ballroom is performed, with movement and costuming meant to be eye-catching, and audience members typically seated on all sides and up to the edge of the dance floor. It is also meant to be creative and expressive, from dancers' choreography and styling to how they dance to a specific piece of music at a specific place and time. Also physically demanding[14] and competitive, dancesport always involves the interplay of each of these dynamics.

Similarly, ballroom competitions are simultaneously festival, celebration, and ritual. While the daily life of most competitors involves varying combinations of teaching and practice, competitions bring together dancers, vendors, and related personnel (such as judges, DJs, MCs, videographers, photographers) from disparate locations.[15] In a related vein, it is not the time learning and rehearsing that are on display, but the dancing 'in the moment' that is performed for audiences and judges. Separate from everyday routines, then, and following their own structure of procedures and personnel, competitions are the places where changes in status are marked and made.

From sporting halls and conference centres to hotel ballrooms to ornate historical venues, ballroom competitions are about the activity and the personnel involved. While different venues contribute different character, being a competitor means producing one's best dancing regardless of the setting. As seen in Figures 5, 6, and 7, there are three interrelated facets of competitions:[16]

• The setting, or *stage*, for the event.
• The *front stage*, on-the-floor performances – including judges and other officials.
• The *backstage*, off-the-floor happenings – including everything from social conversation, sideline naps, handheld videogames, quiet 'head space', disagreements about the dancing, and mental rehearsal all being part of the scene.

The product of all of this is the dancing, which is 1) why my photography became such an important part of my research, and 2) how I came to collect the rich materials for this book.

6. Front stage – Backstage.
Then World and Blackpool Under-21 Latin Finalists, Stas Nikolaev and Kristina Kozlova get what rest they can between rounds as they compete at the 2003 Italian Open. [Colour negatives] © 2003 Jonathan S. Marion.

7. Settings.

Dancesport competitions take place in the 'Ballroom', whether situated in a hotel, sports arena, or event hall. Seen here, competitors practising in the Empress Ballroom at the Winter Gardens facility at the 2013 Blackpool Dance Festival (top); the 2003 Crystal Palace cup being contested at the Crystal Palace National Sport Centre in South London (right); and the hotel ballroom at the 2010 Desert Classic being set up and completed (bottom left and right) in Palm Desert, CA. © 2013, © 2003 [colour negative], and © 2010 Jonathan S. Marion.

Rhythm

Cha Cha, Rumba, Swing, Bolero, and Mambo

Walking into a franchise studio in San Diego, CA in the late 1990s, American Rhythm was the first style I started to learn. In the years ahead, it was also the style I competed in the most: first as an amateur with my then partner Janelle Bouey, and years later in Pro-Am with Carolina Telona (seen with her husband and professional partner, Felipe, in Figures 10, 21, and 27). Long a mainstay of the franchise studios (especially prior to the crumbling of the Iron Curtain and the exodus of many international-style trained Eastern European dancers), American Rhythm is the dancesport style most closely identified with its roots in social dancing. For the dances it shares with International Latin, Rhythm uses slower tempos, and technique-wise involves arriving on a slightly flexed knee, both allowing for fuller body actions. In a related vein, this is the style that allows for the greatest leeway in costuming although in a nod to its social roots, women's skirts are often visibly derivative of non-competition dress, and typically have short hemlines to exhibit leg lines and actions.

8. When it all comes together.
Vince and Alicia Duhon competing at the 2002 Emerald Ball. As soon as I saw the sparkling mesh of Alicia's dress, I knew this was the shot I wanted to get. It was my first image where pose, costume, and setting all came together as a coherent picture. [Colour negative] © 2002 Jonathan S. Marion.

9. Getting into Rhythm.
These were some of the most popular couples on the floor when I started my ballroom research and photography: (clockwise from right) undefeated US Professional Champions Bob Powers and Julia Gorchakova and US Professional Finalists Gleb and Tatiana Makarov competing at the 2002 United States Ballroom Championships, and Professional competitors FJ Abaya and Natasha Thayer at the 2002 Emerald Ball. [Colour negatives] © 2002 Jonathan S. Marion.

10. Felipe and Carolina – my first 'it' shot.
US Professional Finalists Felipe Telona and Carolina Orlovsky-Telona at the 2003 Can-Am Dancesport Gala. This was my first dancesport photo that got any real 'publicity'. To this day people recognize the shot, even if they do not recognize me as the photographer. [Colour negative]
© 2003 Jonathan S. Marion.

11. The Champions.
Later retiring as the 12-time undefeated US Professional Rhythm Champions, Bob Powers and Julia Gorchakova at the 2003 Emerald Ball. [Colour negative]
© 2003 Jonathan S. Marion.

12. Champions say Goodbye.
(This page) Bob Powers and Julia Gorchakova's last competition, at the 2004 United States Dancesport Championships. The inset image shows them atop the podium, just after having had their retirement announcement read by the MC. The emotion in much of the room was palpable, as also seen on the faces of Inna Ivanenko (inset, left) and Carolina Telona (inset, right). [Colour negatives] © 2004 Jonathan S. Marion.

13. Customized Looks.
(Facing page) Showing how the same general costuming conventions get tailored to individual couples 'looks', stylizations, and bodies (clockwise from top left): Professional competitors FJ and Catherine Abaya at the 2004 California Open; Gleb Makarov and May-Ling Hutchins at the 2004 Emerald Ball; Benito Garcia and Anya Fuchs at the 2004 United States Dancesport Championships; and Edgar Osorio and Lori Putnins at the 2004 Yankee Classic. [Colour negatives] © 2004 Jonathan S. Marion.

14. In the Mix.
(Facing page) At the time considered by many to be the next 'it' couple in Rhythm, Professional Finalists Brian Jolly and Kristina Rihanoff at the 2004 United States Dancesport Championships. Kristina is now best known as a professional dancer on *Strictly Come Dancing*, seen here (inset) with fellow *Strictly Come Dancing* professional Matthew Cutler at 'Strictly Come Dancing Live!' at Birmingham National Indoor Arena, February 17, 2009. Main: [colour negative] © 2004 Jonathan S. Marion; below: UK Press via Getty Images (Getty Editorial Image #158113432).

15. Rhythm in Action.
(This page) Choreography, costuming, and performance need to come together to help a couple stand out from the crowd. Unlike most televised versions, dancesport competitions typically find several couples dancing side-by-side, and travelling in and out of the same space on the floor. Seen here, Professional Rhythm competitors Luis Grijalva and Anya Fuchs at the 2005 United States Dancesport Championships. © 2005 Jonathan S. Marion.

16. Variety in Rhythm.
(Facing page) Displaying a variety of approaches to Rhythm costuming and choreography, (clockwise from top left) US Professional Finalists Emmanuel Pierre-Antoine and Joanna Zacharewicz (top, left and right); future National Champions Decho Kraev and Bree Watson; and 2007 US Rising Star Champions Jeremy Gatlin and Anna Harwood at the 2006 United States Dancesport Championships.
© 2006 Jonathan S. Marion.

17. Switching it Up.
(This page) US Professional Champions Jose DeCamps and Joanna Zacharewicz (below) and Finalists Emanuel Pierre-Antoine and Julia Gorchakova (right) in a new partnership for each at the 2007 United States Dancesport Championships. © 2007 Jonathan S. Marion.

18. Lines and Shapes.
Showing a variety of the choreographed lines and shapes that highlight competitive dancing, (counterclockwise from left) US Professional Finalists Emanuel Pierre-Antoine and Julia Gorchakova and 2007 US Professional Rising Star Champions Jeremy Gatlin and Anna Harwood at the 2008 Emerald Ball; and 2008 US Professional Rising Star Champions Edgar Osorio and Mirela Prohaska at the 2008 United States Dancesport Championships. © 2008 Jonathan S. Marion.

19. Fun and Focus.
Demonstrating the in-the-moment focus and performance of fun and ease required by successful competitors, US Professional 9-Dance Vice-Champions, Radomir Pashev and Devorah Kastner, dancing Rhythm at the 2008 United States Dancesport Championships.
© 2008 Jonathan S. Marion.

22. He Frames Her.
In line with the typical ballroom adage that the man is the frame and the woman the art, men's costumes and postures are typically meant to be silhouettes and supports for their partners' movements and more eye-catching attire. Seen here are US Professional Champions Decho Kraev and Bree Watson (left), and Vicechampions Emmanuel Pierre-Antoine and Liana Churilova (below) at the 2010 Emerald Ball. © 2010 Jonathan S. Marion.

23. Coordinated Costuming.
While it is the norm for the man to be in all black, or black trousers and a shirt to match his partner's dress, other approaches to coordinating a couple's costuming also work. Seen here are US Professional Finalists Ilya and Amanda Reyzin (right), Emmanuel Pierre-Antoine and Liana Churilova (below left), and Ricky Bentzen and Albina Habrle (below right) at the 2011 United States Dancesport Championships. © 2011 Jonathan S. Marion.

24. Fitting Together.
Seen here competing in Rhythm at the 2011 United States Dancesport Championships, US Professional 9-Dance Champions Peter and Alexandra Perzhu show how a couple's costuming, body positions, and focus all need to fit together to be successful competitors. © 2011 Jonathan S. Marion.

25. In the Moment.
Whether directed out to the audience or at one's partner, part of good dancing is being emotionally present and focused in one's dancing, as seen here from US Professional Rhythm Finalists and 9-Dance Champions Peter and Alexandra Perzhu (below), and US Professional 9-Dance Vice-champions Sergei Shapoval and Ania Tarnowska (right) at the 2012 United States Dancesport Championships. © 2012 Jonathan S. Marion.

26. Crowd Favourites.
Both overwhelming crowd favourites, US Professional Vice-champions Emmanuel Pierre-Antoine and Liana Churilova (below), and newly switched to Rhythm, US Professional Bronze Medalists, Nazar Norov and Irina Kudryashova (left) at the 2013 United States Dancesport Championships.
© 2013 Jonathan S. Marion.

27. Rhythm Legends.
True champions – as people, friends, and dancers – Felipe and Carolina Telona performing at Dance Legends 2013.
© 2013 Jonathan S. Marion.

Smooth

Waltz, Tango, Foxtrot, and Viennese Waltz

Probably the style most similar to film performances by dancing stars such as Fred Astaire and Ginger Rogers (Figure 28), American Smooth blends social roots with theatrical embellishment. In line with the Hollywood-esque version of the leading man and lady, men typically dance in dinner jackets and women in full-length dresses that are highly embellished both in front and back, and designed to be dramatic, playful, flirtatious, elegant, or some combination that complements the couples' choreography and dance characterizations (how they portray each of the dances). Blending many of the closed-hold techniques of Standard and the open partner-work of Latin (see, for example, Figure 43), Smooth involves the most total movement as partners move both around the floor (progressing counter-clockwise, down the line of dance) but also into and away from each other. Dresses, while long, cannot be too full or have too many extra swaths of streaming fabric as these could easily pose technical difficulties as dancers continuously connect and separate and reconnect.

28. Ginger Rogers and Fred Astaire.
(This page) Seen here during the shooting of the film 'The Gay Divorcee' in 1934, Ginger and Fred helped cement an image and set the tone for this style of ballroom dancing. Similarly, the slim skirt and lack of extraneous elements (which could get tangled during a performance as partners separate and reconnect) – as seen here in Ginger's dress – remain emblematic of contemporary Smooth costuming. © 2012 Getty Images (Photo by AFP/Getty Images, Editorial Image #136396896).

29. Striking Surprise.
(Facing page) Shot on film early in my research, I do not remember taking this image of Professional US Finalists David Weise and Valentina Kostenko at the 2002 Ohio Star Ball. It was a fantastic surprise when I had my negatives developed and started looking through the prints! [Colour negative] © 2002 Jonathan S. Marion.

30. Smooth at Ohio.
(Facing page) The largest competition in the USA is the Ohio Star Ball (OSB), and outside the national championships it is the only competition in the country where almost every national finalist will be on the floor, competing head to head. Unfortunately, the event typically coincides too closely with the American Anthropological Association's annual meeting, so I was only able to attend early in my research. Earlier on, however, it was a crucial stop as it represented the single largest 'in gathering' of North-American dancers, vendors, and officials. Seen here at the 2002 OSB are (clockwise from top left) Professional US Champions Michael Mead and Toni Redpath; Finalists David Weise and Valentina Kostenko; Ben Ermis and Shalene Archer-Ermis; and Nick Kosovich and Lena Bacheva. [Colour negatives] © 2002 Jonathan S. Marion.

31. Competition as Location.
(This page) The competition floor is a location all its own. Regardless of where a particular competition may be held – which state, which city, which venue – the floor is a social and cultural place where dancers perform and form their dancesport identities. Seen here clockwise from right: Ben Ermis and Shalene Archer-Ermis at the 2002 United States Ballroom Championships; US Professional Finalists Hunter Johnson and Maria Zee at the 2002 Pacific Dancesport Championships; and US Professional competitors Jonathan and Melissa Atkinson at the 2002 Pacific Dancesport Championships. [Colour negatives] © 2002 Jonathan S. Marion.

33. Always On.
Whether standing still or mid-movement, once on the competition floor competitors are always performing as seen here from US Professional Finalists Stephen Hevenor and Larinda McRaven (right) and Hunter Johnson and Maria Zee at the 2004 Emerald Ball (below) and at the 2004 United States Dancesport Championships. [Colour negatives]
© 2004 Jonathan S. Marion.

34. Intensity.
(This page) Playful at times, Smooth can also be passionate and intense as showcased by US Professional Champions Nick Kosovich and Lena Bacheva (left) at the 2005 United States Dancesport Championships and US Professional Finalists Hunter Johnson and Maria Zee at the 2005 Desert Classic (below). © 2005 Jonathan S. Marion.

35. Smooth Costuming.
(Facing page) Smooth dresses typically bring together the longer dress style of Standard with the freedom of movement and body display of Latin. Seen here are (clockwise from left) the dance and costume styling of US Professional Champions Ben Ermis and Shalene Archer-Ermis; fellow Professional Finalists Mayo Alanen and Lisa Vogel; Tomas Mielnicki and JT Thomas, seen here at the 2006 Emerald Ball; and Steven Dougherty and Eulia Baranovsky at the 2006 United States Dancesport Championships. © 2006 Jonathan S. Marion.

36. Consummate Performers.
From foot elevation to facial expression, US Professional Champions Tomas Mielnicki and JT Thomas were known for their fun, playful, theatrical style. Seen here (left) at the 2007 United States Dancesport Championships, the inset image shows the deep emotional impact of winning the title. JT may not remember it from amidst the rush of emotions and congratulations, but since I was photographing from the corner of the floor where they exited, I was the first one to hug and congratulate her. © 2007 Jonathan S. Marion.

37. Enjoying the Performance.
US Professional 9-Dance Champions Gunnar and Darryl Sverrison, seen here competing in Smooth at the 2007 United States Dancesport Championships.
© 2007 Jonathan S. Marion.

38. Moods of Smooth.
(Counterclockwise from top)
Showcasing the range of moods viable
across the different Smooth dances –
from fun and playful to straight-faced
and serious – Professional Finalists:
Mayo Alanen and Lisa Vogel at the 2008
Emerald Ball; Eric and Michelle Hudson
at the 2008 San Diego Dancesport
Championships; and John Selby and Irina
Chalkevitch at the 2008 International
Grand Ball. © 2008 Jonathan S. Marion.

39. The Winning Package.
Putting together the look, artistry, and ability, US Professional Smooth Champions Jonathan Roberts and Valentina Kostenko are seen here competing at the 2008 International Grand Ball (below) on their way to winning the National title at the 2008 United States Dancesport Championships. © 2008 Jonathan S. Marion.

40. Smooth Competitors.
(Facing page) Showcasing the range
of styles and approaches to Smooth,
(clockwise from far left) US Professional
Competitors Paul Cloud and Borbala
Bunnett; National Champions Tomas
Mielnicki and JT Damalas; Professional
Finalists and 9-Dance Champions Peter
and Alexandra Perzhu; and title challengers
Slawek Sochacki and Marzena Stachura,
who went on to win the title for the next
four years, all at the 2009 United
States Dancesport Championships.
© 2009 Jonathan S. Marion.

41. Together.
(This page) Synchronized both
emotionally and physically, US
Professional Finalists Mayo Alanen
and Michelle Officer work with and
off of each other to create the shapes
and the emotional connection of their
performance at the 2011 Emerald Ball.
© 2011 Jonathan S. Marion.

43. Blending Both.
Seen here at the 2012 San Diego Dancesport Championships, US Professional Smooth Champions Slawek Sochacki and Marzena Stachura exemplify how Smooth blends the dance skills of Latin (below left) and Standard (below right), skills which they had developed competing in years before (seen here at the same event in 2004). Main: © 2012 Jonathan S. Marion; bottom images: [colour negatives] © 2004 Jonathan S. Marion.

44. Reimagined.
(Facing page) Clearly different from Hollywood versions, Smooth costuming and dance often represent new takes on the leading man and lady image of films gone by. Seen here are US Professional 9-Dance Vice-champions Sergei Shapoval and Ania Tarnowska at the 2013 United States Dancesport Championships, and US Professional Finalists Max Sinitsa and Eulia Baranovsky (inset) at the 2013 Colorado Star Ball. © 2013 Jonathan S. Marion and © 2013 Jonathan S. Marion for DecaDance Photography [Colorado Star Ball].

45. Smooth on Display.
(This page) Performing at Dance Legends 2013, former US Professional Smooth Champions Tomas Mielnicki and JT Damalas showcase both competition (right) and show costuming (below). © 2013 Jonathan S. Marion.

Latin

Cha Cha, Samba, Rumba, Paso Doble, and Jive

International Latin is widely considered the flashiest, most attention-grabbing style of dancesport, including the skimpiest of dresses (women), tightest shirts and trousers (men), and fastest movement. Contrasted with Rhythm, Latin offers faster music tempi, demanding that dancers' straight-leg actions happen faster, producing quicker movement into and out of various body lines and positions. This speed – layered on top of what is often deliberately 'sexy' costuming – produces a product that is easy to appreciate, even without specialized dance training or knowledge. Much further from its social counterparts than Rhythm, Latin often exhibits quite a lot of side-by-side and otherwise separated choreography.

46. US Latin.
(This page, counterclockwise from left)
World and US Professional 10-Dance
Champions Gary and Diana McDonald
and Professional competitors Marcus
Johnson and JT Thomas at the 2002
Emerald Ball. JT later switched to
Smooth, and went on to win the US
title (see Figure 36). US Professional
Finalists Andrew Philips and Katarzyna
Kozak and Maksim Chmerkovskiy and
Elena Grinenko at the 2002 United
States Ballroom Championships. [Colour
negatives] © 2002 Jonathan S. Marion.

47. World Class Latin.
(Facing page) Among the top Latin
dancers in the world when I started my
dancesport research and photography,
(clockwise from left) World and
Blackpool Professional Champions
Bryan Watson and Carmen; and World
and Blackpool Professional Finalists Paul
Killick and Hanna Karttunen and Slavik
Kryklyvyy and Karina Smirnoff at the 2002
United States Ballroom Championships;
and World and Blackpool Professional
Finalists Dmitri Timokhin and Anna
Bezikova at the 2002 German Open
Championships. [Colour negatives]
© 2002 Jonathan S. Marion.

48. Amateur Excellence.

Unlike other activities where professionals are typically far better than amateurs, in dancesport the top tiered amateurs are better than all but the very best of the professionals. Seen here in a variety of amateur partnerships, most of these dancers have gone on to tremendous professional success, either in the competitive or popular arenas. Seen here are (top left) then World and Blackpool Amateur Champions, Franco Formica and Oksana Nikiforova at the 2003 United States Ballroom Championships; (top right) World and Blackpool Amateur Finalists, Evgeni Smagin and Rachael Heron at the 2003 Blackpool Dance Festival; (bottom left) Martino Zanibellato and Michelle Abildtrup – now also the WDSF World Professional Latin Champions – at the 2003 Italian Open; and (near left, above) Under-21 Blackpool Champions, Derek Hough and Aneta Piotrowska at the 2003 Blackpool Dance Festival. Derek is now widely known for his multiple winning seasons as a professional on *Dancing with the Stars* (winning Seasons 7, 10, 11, 16, and 17 with Kristi Yamaguchi, Nicole Scherzinger, Jennifer Grey, Kellie Pickler, and Amber Riley respectively), seen (near left, below) leaving the 'Good Morning America' taping at the ABC Times Square Studios in New York City with Amber Riley on September 4, 2013. [Colour negatives] © 2003 Jonathan S. Marion; inset: © 2013 Ray Tamara/Getty Images (Editorial Image #179508463).

49. Powerful Performers.
World and Blackpool Professional
Finalists Slavik Kryklyvyy and Karina
Smirnoff (right) and Michael Wentink
and Beata Onefater (below left) performing
and competing at the 2003 United States
Ballroom Championships. Karina is now
a household name as a professional on
Dancing with the Stars, including winning
Season 13 with retired soldier and actor
J. R. Martinez – seen (below right) leaving
the 'Good Morning America' taping at the
ABC Times Square Studios in New York City
on November 23, 2011. [Colour negatives]
© 2003 Jonathan S. Marion; © 2011 Ray
Tamara/Getty Images (Editorial Image
#133993940).

50. Apprenticeship on the Floor.
(Clockwise from left) Mark Ballas and Yulia Musikhina at the 2004 United States Dancesport Championships, and at the 2005 Blackpool Dance Festival. Now widely known as a professional on *Dancing with the Stars*, including winning Season 6 (with Kristi Yamaguchi) and Season 8 (with Shawn Johnson). The image below shows Mark performing with Kristi Yamaguchi at the Dizzy Feet Foundation's Inaugural Celebration of Dance at The Kodak Theater on November 29, 2009 in Hollywood, California. Main: [colour negative] © 2004 Jonathan S. Marion; © 2005 Jonathan S. Marion; © 2009 Kevin Winter/Getty Images for Dizzy Feet Foundation (Editorial Image # 93488058).

51. From the Floor to TV.
US Amateur Finalists Alec Mazo and Edyta Śliwińska, seen here competing at the 2004 United States Dancesport Championships (right), as well as at the 2002 Emerald Ball (bottom left). Part of the initial cast of professional dancers on *Dancing with the Stars* in the US, Alec won Season 1 with celebrity partner actress Kelly Monaco (seen bottom right on the ABC 2005 Summer Press Tour) and Edyta danced the most consecutive seasons of any initial cast member, including coming in as runner-up with celebrity partner, NFL Linebacker Jason Taylor (below) in Season 6 (at the Jason Taylor foundation charity Gala dinner, held at the Seminole Hard Rock Hotel and Casino on June 1, 2008 in Hollywood, Florida). Main: [colour negative] © 2004 Jonathan S. Marion; small photos, bottom left: [colour negative] © 2002 Jonathan S. Marion; bottom right: © 2005 Jesse Grant/WireImage (Getty Editorial Image #104814778); below: © 2008 Larry Marano/Getty Images (Editorial Image #81326939).

52. Before TV.
US Professional Finalist
Jonathan Roberts and Anna Trebunskaya,
seen here at the 2004 Emerald Ball,
both went on to have very successful
competitive careers with other partners
and as professionals on *Dancing with
the Stars*. Anna reached third place in
the US Professional Latin dancing with
Pavlo Barsuk (see, for example, Figure
68) and Jonathan went on to win the
US Professional Smooth Championship
dancing with Valentina Kostenko
(see Figure 39). [Colour negative]
© 2004 Jonathan S. Marion.

53. Latin Blondes.
It was only after I had selected these images that I realized each of the women had short blonde hair at the time. An aside in many ways, it has some relevance since Latin – as the dancesport style furthest removed from courtly antecedents – is the ballroom genre where such a haircut is most likely. Seen here are (clockwise from right) future World and Blackpool Professional Champions Michal Malitowski and Joanna Leunis, US Professional Finalists Paul Richardson and Olga Rodionova, and future World and Blackpool Professional Finalists Peter and Kristina Stokkebroe – at the time climbing to be World and Blackpool Amateur Champions – all seen here dancing at the 2004 United States Dancesport Championships. [Colour negatives] © 2004 Jonathan S. Marion.

54. Mixing it Up.
(This page) One of the couples that highlight the unfortunate overall lack of ethnic diversity in dancesport, US Professionals Rick Robinson and Ashley DelGrosso – seen here competing at the 2004 California Open – always seemed to be having fun on the competition floor. Ashley was part of the initial cast of professional dancers when *Dancing with the Stars* first aired in the USA in 2005, placing third with celebrity partner, New Kids on the Block member Joey McIntyre. [Colour negative]
© 2004 Jonathan S. Marion.

55. The Significance of Costuming.
(Facing page) The then World and Blackpool Amateur Vice-champions, later Amateur Champions and Professional Finalists, Klaus Kongsdal and Victoria Franova, seen here at the 2005 Blackpool Dance Festival, including the transformation from 'marking' their routines in practice/street clothes (inset).
© 2005 Jonathan S. Marion.

56. Latin Leaders.
(Clockwise from top left) Providing models for upcoming competitors, World and Blackpool Professional Champions Bryan Watson and Carmen Vicelj and finalists Andrej Skufca and Katarina Venturini, Sergey Ryupin and Elena Khvorova, and Slavik Kryklyvyy and Karina Smirnoff at the 2005 Blackpool Dance Festival. © 2005 Jonathan S. Marion.

57. The Shape of Latin.
Then on their way to being 11-time undefeated US Amateur Champions, Blackpool and World Amateur Finalists – and later US Professional Vice-Champions and Blackpool and World Professional Finalists – Eugene Katsevman and Maria Manusova are seen here at the 2005 Blackpool Dance Festival, performing a flamenco-inspired movement characteristically used in dancing the Paso Doble. © 2005 Jonathan S. Marion.

58. Latin in Motion.
US Professional Latin Finalists
Vaidas Skimelis and Jurga Pupylete,
seen here at the 2005 Yankee Classic
Dancesport Championships. The image
exemplifies the contrast between her
colourful costume and his black one,
and how the cut of her dress highlights
the movement of her dancing. [Colour
negative] © 2005 Jonathan S. Marion.

59. Things Change.

Seen here at the 2005 Embassy Ball, Jose DeCamps and Cheryl Burke became US Professional Latin Semi-finalists in the year they danced together. Jose went on to become the US Professional Rhythm Champion with Joanna Zacharewicz (see, for example, Figures 17 and 21). Cheryl became a household name as a professional on *Dancing with the Stars*, including winning her first and second seasons on the show, with celebrity partners 98 Degrees member Drew Lachey in Season 2 (bottom left, reprising their famous 'Save a Horse, Ride a Cowboy' freestyle routine on the 2007 Dancing with the Stars Tour) and NFL running back Emmitt Smith in Season 3. Now, crossover dance/media celebrities such as Cheryl continue to make regular appearances at a variety of dancesport competitions, but none more so than the Emerald Ball in Los Angeles given timeframe and proximity. Cheryl is seen here with fellow *Dancing with the Stars* professionals Tony Dovalani at the 2010 Emerald Ball (bottom middle) and Nick Kosovich at the 2011 Emerald Ball (bottom right). Main: © 2005 Jonathan S. Marion; bottom left: © 2007 Barry Brechelson/WireImage (Getty Editorial Image # 80318344); bottom middle: © 2010 Jonathan S. Marion; bottom right: © 2011 Jonathan S. Marion.

60. Dressing for Success.
(This page) Then World and Blackpool Amateur finalist, later Amateur Champions and Professional finalists, Maurizio Vescovo and Melinda Torokgyorgy competing at the 2005 Embassy Ballroom Championships. The image below right shows how couples often use different dresses – of similar cut but different colours – to establish 'a look', but still mix things up and draw more attention, as a couple advances between rounds during a competition. Similarly, couples often introduce a new, different look at major competitions, as seen in the contrasting dress style worn by Melinda at Blackpool in 2006 (bottom). © 2005 and © 2006 Jonathan S. Marion.

61. Spectacle at its Best.
(Facing page) US Professional Rising Star Champions Christian Baerens and Kristina Staykova competing at the 2005 United States Dancesport Championships. Since ballroom floors are rectangular, and most of the travelling dances (including all of Standard and Smooth, and two of the five Latin dances) are choreographed to accent the end of a long side of the floor; I typically shoot from one of these corners if that is possible. While this angle provided me with the most consistent results, there can also be magic available when I try different angles: this image is an example. © 2005 Jonathan S. Marion.

63. Power and Performance.
World and Blackpool Professional
Finalists, and US Professional
Champions, Maxim Kozhevnikov
and Yulia Zagoruychenko at the
2007 Blackpool Dance Festival.
© 2007 Jonathan S. Marion.

64. Blackpool Pro Latin.
(Facing page, clockwise from far left)
World and Blackpool Professional
Champions Bryan Watson and Carmen
Vicelj, and Finalists Franco Formica
and Oxana Lebedew, Peter and Kristina
Stokkebroe, and the first competition of
the new partnership of Evgenij Voznyuk
and Oksana Nikiforovaat the 2007
Blackpool Dance Festival.
© 2007 Jonathan S. Marion.

65. Right There.
(This page) World and Blackpool
Professional Finalists Sergey Sourkov
and Agnieszka Menlincka dancing less
than two feet from the front row seats at
the 2007 Blackpool Dance Festival.
© 2007 Jonathan S. Marion.

66. Evoking Emotion.
From intense and intimate connection between partners to exuberant energy directed out to the audience, successful dancesport performances rely on the ability to evoke a range of emotional tones. Seen here are now World Professional Finalists and Blackpool Semi-finalists, Evgeni Smagin and Polina Kazatchenko (left) – 11 months into their partnership as amateurs in this image – and US Professional Finalists Andre and Natalie Paramonov (below) at the 2008 United States Dancesport Championships. © 2008 Jonathan S. Marion.

67. All in the Details.
US Professional Finalists Pavlo Barsuk and Anna Trebunskaya, seen here competing at the 2008 United States Dancesport Championships. From slicked hair to pleasant facial expressions, from white-to-black tone faded fringe, from pointed fingertip to pointed toe, all the details matter.
© 2008 Jonathan S. Marion.

68. Old and New.
2009 and 2010 World (and five-time US National) Professional 10-Dance Champions Gherman Mustuc and Iveta Lukosuite (left) and – seen here in their first competition together – the short-lived professional partnership (documented in the 2011 film *Ballroom Dancer*) of Blackpool Professional Finalists Slavik Kryklyvyy and Anna Melnikova (below left and right). © 2009 Jonathan S. Marion.

69. Monochromatic Impact.
While many competitive costumes are highly colourful, solidly coloured outfits can also have a strong impact – whether matching or offsetting between partners – as seen here (clockwise from right) with World and US Professional Champions Riccardo Cocchi and Yulia Zagoruychenko and Rising Star Finalists Nazar Norov and Irina Kudryashova at the 2010 Emerald Ball, and World and Blackpool Finalists Andrej Skufca and Melinda Torokgyorgy at the 2010 United States Dancesport Championships.
© 2010 Jonathan S. Marion.

71. Showing Up.
To be successful, couples need to 'show up' on the floor – something achieved through both movement and costuming. Seen here are (clockwise from right) US Professional Finalists Nikolai Voronovich and Maria Nikolishina, Andrei Kazlouski and Asta Sigvaldadottir, and Dmitry Kurakin and Violetta Kurakina at the 2012 United States Dancesport Championships. © 2012 Jonathan S. Marion.

72. Tip-to-Tip.
(This page) Commitment to dancing at the highest levels starts off the floor – from costuming and make-up to coif – but comes alive during competition, depending on energy and commitment, to one's partner and to the audience, that goes from fingertip to fingertip, and from toe-tip to toe-tip. Seen here are US Professional Finalists Andre Paramonov and Natalie Paramonov at the 2012 United States Dancesport Championships. © 2012 Jonathan S. Marion.

73. It's All Latin.
(Facing page) Stylistic conventions for movement and costuming apply across all levels of competition, seen here in the dancing of Blackpool (clockwise from top left) Amateur Rising Star Latin Champions Sam Shamseili and Arina Grishanina, Professionals Dmitry Nikishkin and Olena Shvets and Remi Jansen and Debbie Krewinkel, and Blackpool Professional Finalists Stefano Di Filippo and Dasha Chesnokova at the 2013 Blackpool Dance Festival. © 2013 Jonathan S. Marion.

74. Latin Legends.
(Counterclockwise from left, facing page) Seen here performing at Dance Legends 2013, Michal Malitowski and Joanna Leunis, Eugene Katsevman and Maria Manusova , Louis Van Amstel and Julie Fryer and Riccardo Cocchi and Yulia Zagoruychenko. © 2013 Jonathan S. Marion.

Standard

Waltz, Tango, Viennese Waltz, Foxtrot, and Quickstep

International Standard may best be understood as the connoisseurs' style of dancesport. Because partners remain in frame at all times — never separating while dancing — it is hard for a dancesport newcomer to fully grasp and appreciate the range of skills, artistry, and athleticism involved.[1] Closest in style to its courtly upper-class origins, Standard costuming is the most formal and elegant with men wearing black tailsuits and women wearing full-length dresses. Because partners dance in closed-frame, the front of women's bodices may not be as decorated as seen in Smooth dresses, but skirts are often fuller and numerous styles of floats — various swaths of fabric and related elements attached at the woman's wrists and back of the dress — are typical accents that help highlight and enhance progressive and rotational movements as they billow out behind the couple.

75. Getting Started with Standard.
Seen here are World and Blackpool Professional Finalists Massimo Giorgianni and Alessia Manfredini at the 2002 United States Ballroom Championships – the first major event in the US where I was doing ballroom photography. With Standard being the last event of the week, I was running low on film. Also, still being new to dancesport and to ballroom photography, I found Standard the most difficult style to shoot since dancing in frame meant that the couple's heads were often facing in different directions. While I now find this style the easiest to shoot – since the dancers do not separate – I got very few 'good' shots at the outset. [Colour negatives] © 2002 Jonathan S. Marion.

76. World Class Tango.
World and Blackpool Professional
Finalists at the time, later Champions,
Timothy Howson and Joanne Bolton
competing in the 2003 World
Professional Standard Championships
at the 2003 United States Dancesport
Championships (right). Also contesting
the title were World and Blackpool
Professional Finalists William Pino and
Alessandra Bucciarelli (below left) and
Jonathan Wilkins and Katusha Demidova
(below right). The hold for Tango differs
slightly from the other Standard dances,
so the hand positions and some of
the postures and alignments in these
images make it clear what dance is being
performed. All of the dancesport divisions
are replete with similar cues (see, for
example, Figure 57 regarding Paso Doble
in Latin). [Colour negatives] © 2003
Jonathan S. Marion.

77. Champions.
Christopher Hawkins and Hazel Neberry competing and winning the 2003 Blackpool (left) and World (below) Professional Standard Championships respectively at the 2003 Blackpool Dancesport Festival and the 2003 United States Dancesport Championships. [Colour negatives] © 2003 Jonathan S. Marion.

78. From Serious to Smiles.
Different dances, different dancers,
different music, different settings,
and different performances all set the
stage for a variety of expressions and
performed emotions on the dance
floor. (Clockwise from top left) Seen
here are US Professional Semi-finalists
Garry and Rita Gekhman competing
at the 2004 United States Dancesport
Championships; and then World Amateur
Finalists, later World Professional
Finalists, Sascha and Natasha Karabey
and Warren and Kristi Boyce, competing
at the International DanceSport
Federation (IDSF) Grand Slam event
at the 2004 United States Dancesport
Championships. [Colour negatives]
© 2004 Jonathan S. Marion.

79. 'The Shot'.
(Facing page) The then World and Blackpool Amateur Champions (later Professional Finalists) Domenico Soale and Gioia Cerasoli are seen here doing their signature scissor-kick opening pass to their Quickstep routine at the 2005 Embassy Ballroom Championships. From the first time I saw this danced – three years earlier – I knew this was the photograph I wanted to create. When I finally succeeded in capturing this moment, it quickly became my signature dancesport image. Equally highlighting the art and athleticism of competitive ballroom at the highest levels, I regularly use this photograph in my academic writing and presentations. © 2005 Jonathan S. Marion.

80. Heading Forward – One Heel at a Time.
(This page) Progressive steps in Standard (and Smooth) involve a heel lead – having the heel make contact first, and then rolling the body weight forward on to the whole foot. This is clearly seen here, in the dancing of US Professional Finalists Igor Litvinov and Julia Ivleva at the 2005 United States Dancesport Championships. © 2005 Jonathan S. Marion.

81. Preparation and Power.
Whether pushing up on to the balls of the feet in preparation to let gravity help propel the next step (left) or bodily shaping the couple's frame (below), Standard is never static. To the uninitiated outsider the always-closed hold may mask the supreme technique needed to dance in constant body contact at the highest levels, and the floats on Standard dresses help showcase the progression and movement. Seen here are World and Blackpool Professional Finalists William Pino and Alessandra Bucciarelli (left) and then World and Blackpool Amateur Finalists Warren and Kristi Boyce (below) at the 2005 Blackpool Dance Festival. © 2005 Jonathan S. Marion.

82. Taking Standard in Stride.
Seen here at the 2006 Blackpool
Dance Festival, World and Blackpool
Professional Champions Mirko
Gozzoli and Alessia Betti exemplify the
combination of synchronized posture
(notice their straight back lines, with
their heads directly above their spines)
and power (look at their stride length),
as well as the role of the women's dress
in providing a visual cue for the speed
and power of their stride. © 2006
Jonathan S. Marion.

83. Elite Amateur Standard.
(This page, counterclockwise from left) Then Under-21 Semi-finalists Andrey Begunov and Anna Demidova; then World and Blackpool Amateur Finalists – later World IDSF Professional Champions – Paolo Bosco and Silvia Pitton; and fellow Finalists Warren and Kristi Boyce, all at the 2006 Blackpool Dance Festival. © 2006 Jonathan S. Marion.

84. US Standard.
(Facing page, clockwise from right) World and Blackpool Professional Finalists, and US Professional Champions, Jonathan Wilkins and Katusha Demidova; Vice-champions Victor Fung and Anna Mikhed; US Professional Finalists Erminio Stefano and Liene Apale; and later Finalists Urs Geisenhainer and Agnieszka Kazmierczak, all competing at the 2006 United States Dancesport Championships. © 2006 Jonathan S. Marion.

85. Blackpool Standard.
(Facing page, counterclockwise from top right) World and Blackpool Professional Finalists Victor Fung and Anna Mikhed and Domenico Soale and Gioia Cerasoli; Semi-finalists Sascha and Natasha Karabey; and – on the way to winning the Blackpool Amateur Champions' title – Arunas Bizokas and Edita Danuite at the 2007 Blackpool Dance Festival. © 2007 Jonathan S. Marion.

86. Contra Check.
(This page) Seen here at the 2007 United States Dancesport Championships, US Professional Finalists Erminio Stefano and Liene Apale perform a Contra Check: a movement used to stop rotational movements. The degree of preceding rotation is evidenced by how much her dress and his tails wrap around each other. © 2007 Jonathan S. Marion.

87. Standard Champions.
(This page) Now undefeated World and Blackpool Professional Champions, Arunas Bizokas and Katusha Demidova are seen here winning their first US Professional Championship together at the 2008 United States Dancesport Championships. © 2008 Jonathan S. Marion.

88. Variety in Standard.
(Facing page) Although Standard's always-closed hold limits the range of movements possible, how these movements are executed – as well as a vast range of costuming, styling, and performance choices – still provide tremendous variety between couples as seen here in the dancing of (clockwise from right) World Professional 10-dance Champions Gherman Mustuc and Iveta Lukosuite, US Professional Finalists Mikhail Avdeev and Anastasia Muravyova and Urs Geisenhainer and Agnieszka Kazmierczak, and US Professional Semi-finalists Lucas Chockuba and Paulina Malinowska as they all compete at the 2008 United States Dancesport Championships. © 2008 Jonathan S. Marion.

89. Princess.
(This page) Then Professional Rising Star Finalists, Michal Towliszew and Tiffany Fung are seen here competing at the 2009 United States Dancesport Championships. When she first tried on the dress at her sponsor's booth, Tiffany exclaimed that it made her feel like a princess. The serious time and effort behind dancesport training are only part of the picture. Certainly performing 'the fairytale' is part of the picture as well, but there are also those magical moments when one also feels a part of that story. © 2009 Jonathan S. Marion.

90. Displaying Standard.
(Facing page, counterclockwise from right) Seen here at the 2009 United States Dancesport Championships, are US Professional Semi-finalists Lucas Chockuba and Paulina Malinowska, World and US Professional 10-Dance Champions Gherman Mustuc and Iveta Lukosuite, and US Professional Finalists Urs Geisenhainer and Agnieszka Kazmierczak, and, at the 2009 San Diego Dancesport Championships, US Professional Finalists Artem Plakhotnyi and Inna Berlizyeva. © 2009 Jonathan S. Marion.

91. Performing on Tiptoe.
(This page) US Standard Semi-finalists Egor Abashkin and Katya Kanevskaya, seen here (left) at the 2009 United States Dancesport Championships, also seen here (below) at the 2013 United States Dancesport Championships, demonstrate the balance and ankle strength undergirding polished and pleasant performance. © 2009 and 2013 Jonathan S. Marion.

92. Getting There.
(Facing page) Seen dancing here at their first competition together at the 2010 Emerald Ball, Giampiero Giannico and Anna Mikhed went on to place as World and Blackpool Finalists in the six months they competed together. © 2010 Jonathan S. Marion.

93. Performing with Ease.
(This page) Soon to be World and Blackpool Vice-champions, Victor Fung and Anastasia Muravyova are seen here at the 2010 United States Dancesport Championships. The seeming ease with which they perform – seen here in their pleasant facial expressions – belies the effort involved and is a hallmark of excellence in preparation and performance. © 2010 Jonathan S. Marion.

94. Colourful Comparisons.
(Facing page, clockwise from left) World and US National Professional Champions Arunas Bizokas and Katusha Demidova, then third in the World and US Professional National Vice-champions and Victor Fung and Anastasia Muravyova, and US Professional Finalists Mikhail Avdeev and Olga Blinova and Andrey Begunov and Anna Demidova at the 2011 United States Dancesport Championships. © 2011 Jonathan S. Marion.

95. Setting the Standard.
(This page) World, Blackpool, and US National Champions Arunas Bizokas and Katusha Demidova at the 2012 United States Dancesport Championships. © 2012 Jonathan S. Marion.

96. On the Blackpool Floor.
(Clockwise from right) US Professional Finalists Mikhail Avdeev and Olga Blinova, Blackpool Professional Finalists Chao Yang and Yiling Tan, and British Professional Champions Warren and Kristi Boyce at the 2013 Blackpool Dance Festival. © 2013 Jonathan S. Marion.

97. Standard Legends.
(Counterclockwise from left) Standard legends WDSF World Professional Champions Mirko Gozzoli and Edita Daniute, WDSF World Amateur Champions Emanuel Valeri and Tania Kehlet, WDC World Champions Arunas Bizokas and Katusha Demidova and WDC World Vice-champions Victor Fung and Anastasia Muravyova (facing page), at Dance Legends 2013. © 2013 Jonathan S. Marion.

End notes

Acknowledgements
1   See Marion 2008:ix for a partial listing.

Photographing Ballroom
1   For examples see Marion 2006, Marion 2008, and Ericksen 2011.
2   See Marion 2008, Introduction.
3   Years later, I returned to the floor to compete with my instructor in Pro-Am.
4   See Marion 2010.
5   See McMains 2006, Marion 2008, Ericksen 2011, Marion and Crowder 2013.
6   For more on visual ethics see: Perry and Marion 2010, and Marion and Crowder 2013 (especially Chapter 1).
7   See Marion 2010 and Marion 2012 for ballroom-based, article-length photo-essays.
8   See Radler 1996 and Marion 2008, Chapter 3.
9   See Marion 2011.
10   See anthropologist and commercial photographer Richard Freeman, (Freeman 2009:59).
11   My idea of the ballroom world comes from sociologist Howard Becker's concept of the art world (Becker 1984, and Becker 2001) and anthropologist Helena Wulff's extension of this to the ballet world (Wulff 1998).
12   See Marion 2012 regarding the ongoing circuits of competitive ballroom dance.

13   See Marion 2008 (especially Chapter 9), Marion 2013a, Marion 2013b, and Ericksen 2011 regarding ballroom costuming.
14   See Bateson 1972:134,137.

Ballroom Dancing: An Introduction
1   See Marion 2008, Marion 2013a, and Ericksen 2011.
2   See, for example, Arbeau 1589/1967.
3   Although not widely recognized within the larger dancesport arena, wheelchair dancesport takes place under the auspices of the International Paralympic Wheelchair Dance Sport Committee (IPWDSC), and dancesport has emerged as one of the most popular events at the gay games (with different divisions for men and women).
4   Such as Street Latin and New Vogue in Australia, and cabaret, theatre arts, and Classic and Latin American showadance worldwide.
5   A shortened version of the original name, Latin and American.
6   Also known as Ballroom or Modern.
7   Adapted form Marion 2008:24.
8   In Pro-Am events several other dances may be included as 'Rhythm'. Strictly speaking, however, it is the five dances listed here that constitute the competitive style.
9   As noted in Marion 2008:26.
10   See, for example, Vermey 1994 and McMains 2006.

11   See Marion 2013a.
12   Marion 2008, Chapters 4–8.
13   Borrowing from McAloon's (1984) conceptualization of the modern Olympics as a meta-genre of spectacle, festival, ritual, and game.
14   See, for example, Blanksby and Reidy 1988, Bria et al. 2011, and Prosen et al. 2013.
15   See Marion 2012.
16   Borrowing from Goffman's (1959/1990) dramaturgical model.

Standard
1   Indeed, when I first started photographing ballroom, I found this style the most difficult, as both partners were rarely facing the same direction (and I prefer to get both faces wherever possible). Now, after years of exposure, knowledge, and understanding, I typically find this style the easiest to photograph.

Appendix

Event names and locations
Blackpool Dance Festival: Blackpool, England
California Open: Costa Mesa, CA
California Star Ball: Los Angeles, CA
Can-Am Dancesport Gala: Toronto, Canada.
Colorado Star Ball: Westminster, CO
Crystal Palace Cup: South London, England
Dance Legends: New York, NY
Desert Classic: Palm Desert, CA.
Embassy Ballroom Championships: Irvine, CA
Emerald Ball: Los Angeles, CA
German Open Championships: Mannheim, Germany
Holiday Dance Classic: Las Vegas, NV
International Grand Ball: San Francisco, CA
Italian Open Championships: Cervia, Italy
Ohio Star Ball: Columbus, OH
Pacific Dancesport Championships: Los Angeles, CA
San Diego Dancesport Championships: San Diego, CA
United States Ballroom Championships: Miami, FL
   Changed to United States Dancesport Championships: Hollywood Beach, and then Orlando, FL
Yankee Classic: Boston, MA

References

Arbeau, T. (1589/1967), *Orchesography*. Translated by M. Stewart Evans, edited by J. Sutton. New York: Dover.

Bateson, G. (1972), *Steps to an Ecology of Mind*. New York: Ballantine Books.

Becker, H.S. (1984), *Art Worlds*. Berkeley: University of California Press.

Becker, H.S. (2001), 'Art as Collective Action', in C. Lee Harrington and D.D. Bielby (eds) *Popular Culture: Production and Consumption*. Malden, MA: Blackwell Publishers Inc.

Blanksby, B.A. and Reidy, P.W. (1988), 'Heart Rate and Estimated Energy Expenditure During Ballroom Dancing', *British Journal of Sports Medicine*, 22(2): 57–60.

Bria, S., Bianco, M., Galvani, C., Palmieri, V., Zeppilli, P. and Faina, M. (2011), 'Physiological Characteristics of Elite Sport-Dancers', *The Journal of Sports Medicine and Physical Fitness*, 51(2): 194–203.

Ericksen, J. (2011), *Dance With Me: Ballroom Dancing and the Promise of Instant Intimacy*. New York: NYU Press.

Freeman, R. (2009) 'Photography and Ethnography', in M. Strong and L. Wilder (eds), *Viewpoints: Visual Anthropologists at Work,* Austin: UT Press.

Goffman, E. (1959/1990), *The Presentation of Self in Everyday Life*, London: Penguin Books.

Marion, J.S. (2006), *Dance as Self, Culture, and Community: The Construction of Personal and Collective Meaning and Identity in Competitive Ballroom and Salsa*, Ph.D. Dissertation, La Jolla, CA: University of California San Diego.

Marion, J.S. (2008), *Ballroom: Culture and Costume in Competitive Dance*, Oxford: Berg.

Marion, J.S. (2010), 'Photography as Ethnographic Passport', *Visual Anthropology Review*, 26(1): 24–30.

Marion, J.S. (2011), 'Introduction to Photographing an Emotion', in J. Ericksen (ed) *Dance With Me: Ballroom Dancing and the Promise of Instant Intimacy*, New York: NYU Press.

Marion, J.S. (2012), 'Circulation as Destination: Considerations from the Translocal Culture of Competitive Ballroom Dance', *Journal for the Anthropological Study of Human Movement*, 17(2).

Marion, J.S. (2013a), 'Competitive Ballroom Dance', *Berg Encyclopedia of World Dress and Fashion: Volume 10*, Berg Fashion Library Online.

Marion, J.S. (2013b), 'Snapshot: Ballroom Practice Dress', *Berg Encyclopedia of World Dress and Fashion: Volume 10*, Berg Fashion Library Online.

Marion, J.S. (2013c), 'Contextualizing Content and Conduct in the LA and West Coast Salsa Scenes' in S. Hutchinson (ed.), *Salsa World: A Global Dance in Local Contexts*, Temple University Press.

Marion, J.S. (2014), 'Seeing and Being in Contemporary Orthodox Jewish Dress', in N. Valman and L. Roth (eds), *The Routledge Companion to Contemporary Jewish Cultures*, Routledge.

Marion, J.S. and Crowder, J.W. (2013), *Visual Research: A Concise Introduction to Thinking Visually*, London: Bloomsbury.

McAloon, J. (1984), 'Olympic Games and the Theory of Spectacle', in J. McAloon (ed.) *Rite, Drama, Festival, Ritual: Rehearsals Toward a Theory of Cultural Performance*, Philadelphia: Institute for the Study of Human Issues.

McMains, J. (2006), *Glamour Addiction: Inside the American Ballroom Industry*, Middletown, Connecticut: Wesleyan.

Perry, S. and Marion, J.S. (2010), 'State of the Ethics in Visual Anthropology?', *Visual Anthropology Review*, 26(2): 96–104.

Prosen, J., James, N., Dimitriou, L., Perš, J. and Vučković, G. (2013), 'A Time-Motion Analysis of Turns Performed by Highly Ranked Viennese Waltz Dancers', *Journal of Human Kinetics*, 37: 55–62.

Radler, D. (1996), 'How a Dance Competition Is Judged', available at http://www.ballroomdance.net/How_a_Competition_is_Judged_.html (accessed 27 June 2013).

Vermey, R. (1994), *Latin: Thinking Sensing and Doing in Latin American Dancing*. Munich: Kastell Verlag.

Wulff, H. (1998), *Ballet Across Borders: Career and Culture in the World of Dancers*. New York: Berg.